Searchlight BOOKS™

What Can We Learn from Early Civilizations?

Tools and Treasures of

Ancient Mesopotamia

Matt Doeden

Lerner Publications Company
Minneapolis

Lerner Publications Company
A division of Lerner Publishing Group, Inc.
241 First Avenue North
Minneapolis, MN 55401 U.S.A.

For reading levels and more information, look up this title at www.lernerbooks.com.

Library of Congress Cataloging-in-Publication Data

Doeden, Matt.
    Tools and treasures of ancient Mesopotamia / by Matt Doeden.
        pages   cm. — (Searchlight books : what can we learn from early civilizations?)
    Includes index.
    ISBN 978–1–4677–1432–7 (lib. bdg. : alk. paper)
    ISBN 978–1–4677–2507–1 (eBook)
    1. Iraq—Civilization—To 634—Juvenile literature. I. Title.
DS69.5.D64 2014
935—dc23   2013018664

Manufactured in the United States of America
1 — PC — 12/31/13

Contents

Chapter 1

ANCIENT MESOPOTAMIA

Six thousand years ago, human beings lived mostly as hunters and gatherers. They moved from place to place in search of food. But in one small area, life was about to change forever. Between the Tigris and Euphrates Rivers in modern-day Iraq, civilization was beginning.

These ruins are in modern-day Iraq. How long ago did civilization begin here?

The First Civilization

People in the area began to farm the land. With farms to tend to, they could settle in one place. They were leaving their hunting and gathering lifestyle behind. This group of people was becoming the world's first civilization. Later on, the area where they lived was called Mesopotamia.

The ancient Greeks named the area between the Tigris and the Euphrates *Mesopotamia*. The word means "the land between two rivers."

The Tigris and the Euphrates Rivers flooded every year. Mesopotamians learned to manage these floods. They built canals to direct floodwaters to the lowlands. The floods watered the land and brought rich soil.

Modern Iraqis still use canals to manage the Tigris and Euphrates Rivers.

This Mesopotamian art shows someone planting and tending crops.

People figured out how to plant and grow crops in the soil. Farming gave them a steady food supply. Villages formed. Some of them grew into the first cities.

Around 3500 BCE, the culture near the cities of Ur and Uruk changed suddenly. No one knows exactly why. But the cities' population grew very quickly. The people in these cities lived and worked together.

A man and a child stand in the ruins of Uruk.

Ancient Mesopotamia

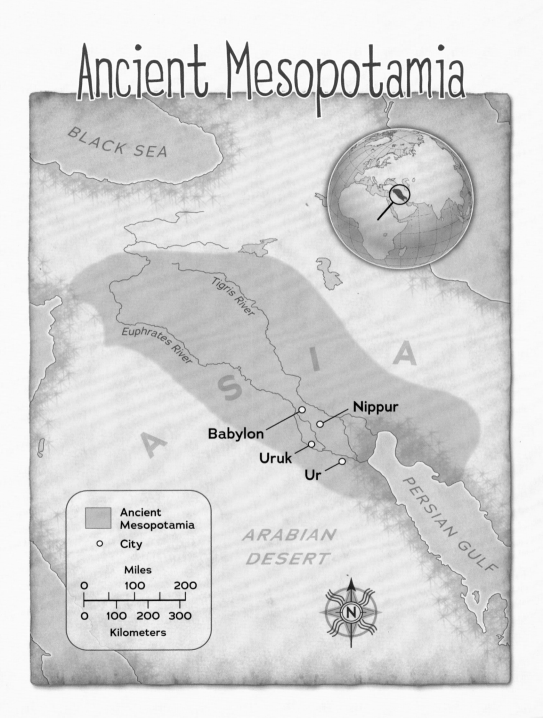

BLACK SEA

Tigris River

Euphrates River

A S I A

Nippur

Babylon

Uruk

Ur

ARABIAN DESERT

PERSIAN GULF

Ancient Mesopotamia

○ City

Miles

0   100   200

0   100 200 300

Kilometers

N

This society was called Sumer. The people who lived there were the Sumerians. People in this culture invented the first system of writing. They produced the first written history. Soon they wrote the first literature.

Many museums display Sumerian artifacts. These artifacts come from Uruk. Uruk is the earliest city scientists have found.

Empires Rise and Fall

More cities rose in Mesopotamia. Each city and the lands it controlled was called a city-state. The city-states often fought with one another. Empires rose and fell.

Around 2000 BCE, a group called the Amorites invaded. They wiped out the Sumerians. The Amorites took control of much of Mesopotamia. Another group called the Assyrians also moved in.

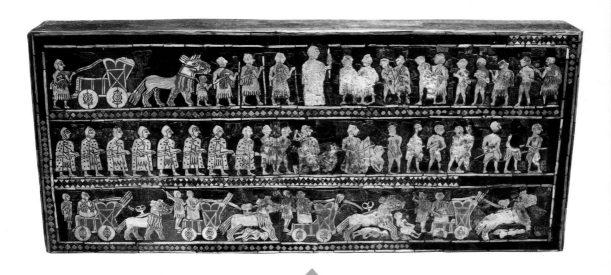

THIS ANCIENT MOSAIC SHOWS
PICTURES OF SUMERIAN WARS.

In the 1700s BCE, Babylon was the most powerful city in Mesopotamia. Its ruler was Hammurabi. He joined all of Mesopotamia together. Babylon ruled the region for more than a hundred years. But Babylon also fell to invaders. Groups including the Hittites and the Assyrians took over the land.

Hammurabi was one of the first rulers to write laws for his people.

Over thousands of years, many empires ruled Mesopotamia. Each empire borrowed from the one before it. They copied parts of the previous empire's art, writing, religion, and more. Much of what the Sumerians established was handed down through the centuries. Many of their ideas lived on in Mesopotamia long after they were gone.

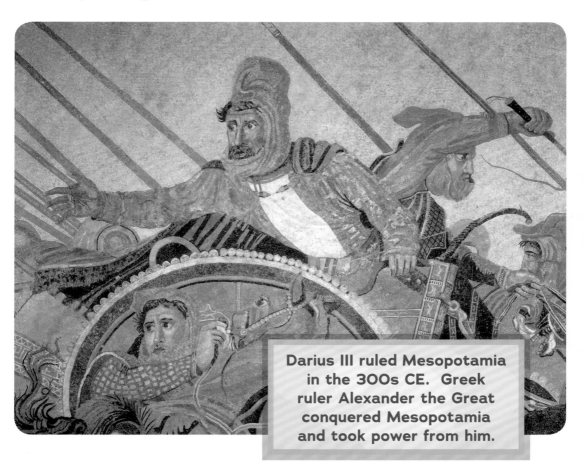

Darius III ruled Mesopotamia in the 300s CE. Greek ruler Alexander the Great conquered Mesopotamia and took power from him.

Chapter 2

DAILY LIFE

Life changed when the first civilization rose. People didn't have to spend all their time searching for food. Some people grew food, while other people hunted. Other members of society made things. Then they traded these goods with one another.

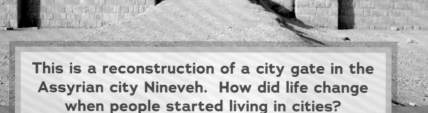

This is a reconstruction of a city gate in the Assyrian city Nineveh. How did life change when people started living in cities?

Mesopotamian people had time to develop art and writing and to invent new tools. A class system began. Kings were at the top. They ruled over the common people. Slaves were at the bottom. They did the hardest jobs for no pay.

In this carving, the Assyrian king Ashurnasirpal (RIGHT) is on his way to a hunt.

Work

Farmers in Mesopotamia grew wheat and barley. They also farmed peas, carrots, and onions. Farmers used tools such as plows and sharp blades to plant and harvest crops. Pigs, goats, and sheep were raised for food and wool. Strong oxen and donkeys pulled plows.

THIS SEAL SHOWS FARMERS GUIDING AN OX THROUGH A FIELD.

These gold daggers belonged to a Sumerian ruler in the 2000s BCE. He probably displayed them during ceremonies.

Other Mesopotamian people were craftsmen. They made kitchen tools, shovels, and weapons out of copper, bronze, and iron.

Communication

Over the years, the people of Mesopotamia spoke many languages. Many city-states had their own languages. The main language early on was Sumerian. Later, Akkadian took over. The people of Mesopotamia traded with one another and with other cultures. As a result, many of them spoke two or more languages.

Some children learned to read and write. This tablet was used for schoolwork.

The Sumerians used writing to record trades and keep track of crops. They could send written messages. Kings could write down the laws of the land. The invention of writing was a big part of what made them the first civilization.

PEOPLE ALSO WROTE DOWN
INFORMATION FOR BUSINESS.

Writing allowed the Sumerians to record their own history. Much of what we know about ancient people comes from their own writing. Before the Sumerians, people probably talked and traded goods. But no one knows exactly how. They left no record of it. The invention of writing changed that.

Babylonians trade at a marketplace in this modern painting.

Few common people could read and write. That job went to trained scribes. The earliest form of writing used pictures to represent objects. Later, scribes used symbols to represent words.

Most scribes were men, but a few of them were women.

Scribes wrote on clay tablets. They used a writing tool called a stylus to press words into wet clay. When the scribe was done writing, he baked the clay tablet in an oven. This set the clay and preserved the writing. Many of these clay tablets have survived to the modern day in good condition!

This modern re-creation of a stylus and a clay tablet shows how these tools worked.

Religion

People in Mesopotamia worshipped many gods. They believed that the gods controlled the weather, the growth of crops, and more. The people honored the gods by building temples and carving stone statues of the gods. People sometimes prepared food and offered it to the gods.

Marduk was the most important Mesopotamian god. He was often drawn or sculpted as a dragon.

Priests were among the most powerful people in Mesopotamia. Mesopotamians believed that priests could talk with the gods. Priests and kings worked together to govern cities.

The king and two minor gods bring offerings to Shamash, the sun god.

Chapter 3

THE CULTURE OF ANCIENT MESOPOTAMIA

A new culture grew with the rise of Sumer. The culture changed as new empires rose and fell. But much of what the Sumerians created remained. Their religion, art, and architecture all shared common characteristics.

This Assyrian ivory carving is from the 700s BCE. What culture did Assyrian culture grow out of?

Art

Some of the oldest surviving art in the world came from Mesopotamia. Sculptures carved in stone or metal showed leaders and gods. Artists also created small stone cylinder seals. The surfaces of the seals were carefully carved. The owner of a cylinder seal pressed it onto a clay tablet and rolled it. The result was a special pattern that identified the owner.

The stone seal on the left created the clay tablet on the right.

Clay pottery was also common. Potters used slowly spinning wheels to create a wide variety of pots, bowls, dishes, and more. Around 1600 BCE, the Mesopotamians learned to blow glass. They produced fine vases, bottles, and other objects.

Mesopotamians were the first people to produce glass vases.

Another kind of Mesopotamian art that still survives is jewelry. Women and men both wore necklaces, ankle bracelets, and earrings. Sometimes statues wore jewelry too! People thought gemstones kept sickness and bad spirits away.

Gold pendants hang from this gemstone necklace.

No one knows what music in ancient Mesopotamia sounded like. But we do know that musicians played many instruments. These included drums and stringed instruments such as the harp.

ASSYRIAN MUSICIANS PLAY HARPS AND FLUTES IN THIS STONE CARVING.

Architecture

Most buildings in Mesopotamia were made from bricks fashioned from dried mud. These buildings were short and simple. Even a king's palace was fairly small. That's because the mud bricks weren't very strong. They could not support a huge, heavy structure.

Mesopotamians used mud bricks to build this palace.

This drawing shows a ziggurat. Its highest, smallest level is a temple.

Each city had a huge building called a ziggurat. This building was made up of many stacked platforms of solid mud brick. The platforms got smaller and smaller toward the top. At the very top stood a temple. Temples were designed to be homes for the gods.

Pastimes

The people of Mesopotamia enjoyed their free time. Athletes wrestled, ran footraces, and held archery contests. Some people kept dogs and birds as pets. Board games were popular, especially backgammon. Players threw dice and moved pieces around a board. Backgammon sets more than five thousand years old have survived to this day!

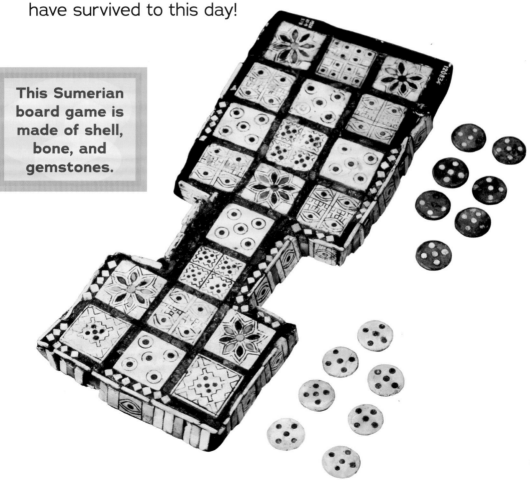

This Sumerian board game is made of shell, bone, and gemstones.

Mesopotamian Folklore

Gilgamesh

The most famous story from Mesopotamia is the Epic of Gilgamesh. It tells the tale of a great king who was part man, part god. His story is very long. Here is a small part.

Gilgamesh is the king of the city of Uruk. But he is bored there. So he and his friend Enkidu leave in search of adventure. On their journey, they find an ogre named Humbaba.

Humbaba teases Gilgamesh. Humbaba promises to kill him and feed him to the birds. Gilgamesh is afraid. But Enkidu convinces him to fight. A great battle follows. The sky darkens, and the mountains shake. The gods send wind to help Gilgamesh trap Humbaba. Gilgamesh takes pity on the ogre and decides not to kill him. But when Humbaba curses the two men, Gilgamesh grows angry. He lashes out and kills the ogre.

Gilgamesh and Enkidu cut down trees to make a raft. Then they return home on the Euphrates River, carrying the head of Humbaba on their raft.

Chapter 4

MESOPOTAMIA TODAY

Mesopotamia's fertile land made it a target for attacking forces. Sumer, Assyria, and Babylon all rose and fell to attacking armies. Over thousands of years, Mesopotamia was ruled by at least a dozen different empires.

Workers clean an Assyrian statue at a site in Iraq. Which other empires ruled Mesopotamia?

In the 600s CE, Arab armies conquered Mesopotamia. They brought with them the religion of Islam. Islam took over as the area's main religion. It remains so in modern times.

Arabs built this minaret in the 800s CE. Minarets call Muslims to prayer.

Iraq

In the early 1900s, the Ottoman Empire ruled the area once known as Mesopotamia. The empire was destroyed in World War I (1914–1918). A new nation called Iraq was created. Iraq included most of the lands that had been home to Sumer, Babylon, and other Mesopotamian Empires.

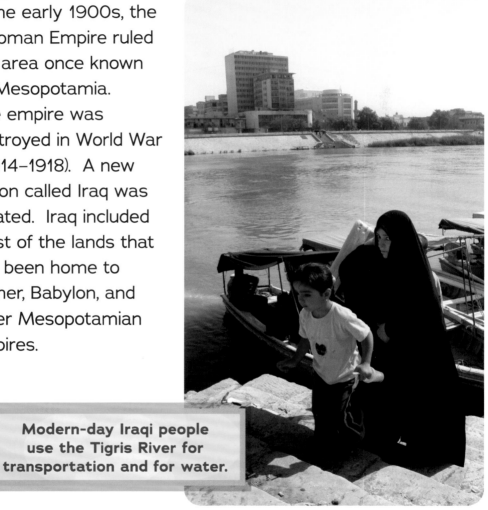

Modern-day Iraqi people use the Tigris River for transportation and for water.

The Tigris River flows through modern-day Baghdad, Iraq.

Modern-day Iraq is home to more than 30 million people. Many are the descendants of ancient Mesopotamians. The ancient cultures may be long gone. But some of their art, writing, and architecture survives. These treasures remind the people of Iraq of the great civilizations that thrived there thousands of years ago.

Glossary

backgammon: a board game invented in Mesopotamia and still played in modern times

canal: an artificial waterway, often used to bring water to cropland

city-state: a self-governing city and the lands it controls

civilization: a large society in which people share a common government and culture

conquer: to take over a land by force

scribe: a person in ancient times who was specially trained to read and write

ziggurat: a temple shaped like a pyramid, with a large platform at the bottom and gradually smaller platforms going up

LERNER
e
SOURCE

Expand learning beyond the printed book. Download free, complementary educational resources for this book from our website, www.lernerresource.com.

Learn More about Ancient Mesopotamia

Books

Apte, Sunita. *Mesopotamia*. New York: Children's Press, 2010. Why was Mesopotamia home to the world's first civilizations? How did the Mesopotamians build a huge garden in the desert? Find out the answers to these questions and more in this factual look at Mesopotamia.

Kerrigan, Michael. *Mesopotamians*. New York: Marshall Cavendish Benchmark, 2010. Read what the Mesopotamian people had to say about themselves in this collection of historical writings from ancient times.

Rustad, Martha E. H. *The Babylonians: Life in Ancient Babylon*. Minneapolis: Millbrook Press, 2010. Find out what life in ancient Babylon was like with the photographs and vivid comic-style illustrations in this book.

Websites

Ancient Mesopotamia for Kids
http://mesopotamia.mrdonn.org
Read about daily life in Mesopotamia, including school, laws, inventions, and other fascinating topics.

The British Museum—Mesopotamia
http://www.mesopotamia.co.uk/menu.html
Explore drawings and play games to understand the daily challenges ancient Mesopotamians faced.

National Geographic Kids: **Mesopotamia**
http://video.nationalgeographic.com/video/kids/people-places-kids /iraq-mesopotamia-kids
Watch this video history from *National Geographic* to learn about Mesopotamian laws, literature, and engineering.

Index

Photo Acknowledgments

The images in this book are used with the permission of: © David Lees/CORBIS, p. 4; © Adam Ashton/MCT via Getty Images, p. 5; © Nik Wheeler/Alamy, p. 6; © Erich Lessing/Art Resource, NY, pp. 7, 15, 18, 29, 32; © Nik Wheeler/CORBIS, p. 8; © Laura Westland/Independent Picture Service, p. 9; AP Photo/Markus Schreiber, p. 10; © Kmiragaya/Dreamstime.com, p. 11; © Ancient Art & Architecture Collection Ltd/Alamy, p. 12; © Roman/The Bridgeman Art Library/Getty Images, p. 13; © Imagestate Media Partners Limited - Impact Photos/Alamy, p. 14; © Werner Forman/ Universal Images Group/Getty Images, p. 16; © Robert Harding Picture Library/SuperStock, pp. 17, 35; © Prisma/Album/SuperStock, p. 19; Album/Art Resource, NY, p. 20; © Gianni Dagli Orti/The Art Archive at Art Resource, NY, p. 21; © Steve Gorton/Dorling Kindersley/Getty Images, p. 22; © The Bridgeman Art Library/Getty Images, pp. 23, 30; © Universal Images Group/SuperStock, p. 24; © Werner Forman/CORBIS, p. 25; © A. DE GREGORIO/De Agostini/Getty Images, pp. 26, 28; Adam Woolfitt/Robert Harding/Newscom, p. 27; © DEA PICTURE LIBRARY/De Agostini/Getty Images, p. 31; © DeAgostini/SuperStock, p. 33; © KARIM SAHIB/AFP/Getty Images, p. 34; AP Photo/Samir Mizban, p. 36; © Lynsey Addario/VII/CORBIS, p. 37.

Front Cover: © DeAgostini/SuperStock.

Main body text set in Adrianna Regular 14/20. Typeface provided by Chank.